THOUGHTS

ON THE

PRESENT CRISIS.

[*Reprinted from the* LITERARY CHURCHMAN, *June* 6, 1874.]

LONDON :

W. SKEFFINGTON, 163 PICCADILLY, W.

—

1874.

THOUGHTS

ON THE

PRESENT CRISIS.

BEFORE these lines meet our readers' eyes the debate in Committee on the Primates' Bill will have recommenced in the House of Lords, and some probable forecast may perhaps by that time be possible of the course which things will take. While we write the debate is still suspended, so that any remarks of ours may perhaps be already antiquated by the time that they are printed. Yet, so serious is the situation, that we have not the heart to take up any other subject while this yet presses. We are not alarmists. Our readers will at least do us thus much justice—that we are not in the habit of magnifying differences, difficulties, or dangers. Yet we must confess that the present crisis does strike us as, to say the least, the gravest crisis which the Church of England has had to face within the last five-and-twenty years. The mischief is that the danger comes from within. So long as it was merely from Miallites and Liberation Society people that our difficulties arose, we had always this to fall back upon, that a Church which did its work might smile at outside enemies. But now it is from within that the danger comes; and what makes it tenfold bitterer is that the arrow which carries the harm is aimed at her by those who ought to be her guides and her protectors. It is her own Archbishops who strike the blow. We say Archbishops, for, *as a body*, the collective Episcopate follows in unwilling silence. Some among the Bishops there are who concur *ex animo* with their Archiepiscopal chiefs. But speaking of them as a body, they know too much of the state of the Church not to foresee the grave evils which impend. They know also too well the whirlpool of turmoil in which they will themselves be plunged if such a Bill passes to look with any complaisance upon its working. Yet, with one* or two exceptions, they follow like sheep to the slaughter and make no sign. We only hope that our simile is not going to be verified, and that it is not to the slaughter of themselves but only to that of the Bill that they are thus following. But at any rate, if the Bill be ultimately killed, it will not be their doing; though we believe that no rejoicings over its destruction will be more fervent than those of some of our silent Fathers in God. Yet, as a body, they allow it to be said that the Bill rejoices in the concurrence of the Bench, as well as in the promotion of the Archbishops. Verily if the Church Establishment of England is to be wounded to the death it will be by an arrow feathered from its own wing!

---

* Notably the Bishop of Lincoln. See his admirable pamphlet— 'A Plea for Toleration by Law.' London: Rivingtons. Pp. 13. Price 2d.

It is the more bitter, too, because hitherto we have been accustomed to consider that Bishops and Archbishops sat in the House of Lords as the official representatives, and therefore champions, of the Church in the secular Legislature. In the House of Commons the clergy have no representation; Church matters in that house have to depend on the chance of there being some laymen willing to get up the case. But in the House of Lords, we have been always told that the needful counterpoise existed in the presence of the Episcopal experts who were officially *on fait* with matters religious and ecclesiastical. Now this security breaks down, and breaks down utterly. An Archbishop who has never held a parish, whose clerical experience is absolutely *nil*, whose knowledge of clerical matters must be a *minimum* if we are to judge by his speech in the House of Lords on the 20th April;—it is an Archbishop who introduces a Bill which must make the Establishment unworkable, and scarely a Bishop is found to expose the danger. What a commentary on the often quoted warning—" Put not your trust in Princes." The one plea for the Bishops of the Church being Peers of Parliament as well is found to fail us, and not only so but our own supposed defence is turned into our danger. We cannot conceive the possibility of such a Bill having been introduced into Parliament with the smallest chance of success had the House consisted of laymen only. Suppose the Bishops had *not* been Peers. Suppose that a Government had been so misguided as to think of such a Bill. Why then the Government would, as a matter of course, have

consulted the parties concerned, and would have taken
good care to avoid the rocks which would have been
pointed out to it. But now the Government and the
lay portion of the House can say to us—" It is your
" own natural and official leaders who say the Bill is
" necessary, and it is only decent in us laymen to
" listen to your Bishops."

Yet it is a Bill which must split the Establishment
if it passes. We see no hope. It will make the
Establishment unworkable. Not perhaps in a day or
two. For on the whole the existing race of clergy
have a far stronger hold on their parishes than the
Primates imagine, and the difficulties of the last few
years have in a vast number of cases trained the
clergy to hold their own, and thus have given them
an amount of moral force even in ill-conditioned
parishes which will keep things in much better order
than some alarmists think. But though men may hold
their own there will result a chronic state of soreness,
suspicion, and unrest which will bear down the firmest
spirits and do more damage to the proper spiritual
work of the clergy than can well be estimated. With
Archbishops putting a premium upon disaffection to
the clergy, parishes which are contented will begin to
think it is a reflection upon them if they do not find
something to grumble at. The *mauvais sujets* of a
parish will reproach their contented fellow-parishioners
with being slow, priest-led, and stupid. Every word
or look or gesture on the parson's part will be supposed to be the precursor of his beginning to do some
thing which will want watching, and parochial peace
will have vanished for ever. Add to this the Arch-

Bishop's peculiar affection for non-communicants and for extending the right of parson-baiting even to non-residents, so that the incumbent who carries with him every churchman in his parish is to be exposed to attack if there can be found three Dissenters who own property therein, and we see at once how easily, as time goes on, the position of an incumbent may be made untenable. The Liberation Society has nothing to do but to stir up a few Dissenters in every considerable parish and the thing is done. Nay, if there be a parish where there are none, it has only to buy a few tenements, put in a few of its own creatures as freeholders, and commence a war of worry. Of course it is easy to say that the Bishops need not sanction suits. But this will prove a very flimsy defence when the time comes. Hitherto the real security for a clergyman's devoting himself to his proper spiritual duties has been his exemption from exterior worries. A man cannot be always either actually fighting or expecting to have to fight with the wild beasts of " aggrieved parishioners," and at the same time efficient in pastoral visitation, and devoted to spiritual studies. But this is what the Archbishop will bring him to. And so, supposing that the existing race of clergy manage to hold their own for a while, by force of personal character and power, still *their office must come into disrepute*. The parishioner's idea of a clergyman will come to be that of an official person, who is always either being baited, or going to be baited, and that by the lowest and least respected, or at all events by the most cantankerous of the people. The *prestige* of the office must go. If you, as an individual, have already gained the respect of your parish, *you* may succeed in keeping it, in spite of all. But woe be to the man that comes after you : and woe be to you if you exchange your present cure for a town parish where you are not known, and have your *prestige* to win. The Archbishop is destroying the clerical position, and we would like to know when that is gone what there is to draw the supply of future clergy? Of course there will always be some men of high power and lofty character who will be found in the ministry of the Church, even if she be in her uttermost degradation. It is in the darkest hours that the brightest lights shine brightest. But we are speaking of the average men, and of the average positions. And in such cases as these it is that this baiting-made-easy of the parsons will tell so fatally. It is already the cry that the smallness of clerical incomes makes it difficult to get clergy enough. But how will it be if besides the smallness of the remuneration you have also the destruction of the position, or rather the position rendered one which will be,— *first,*—intolerable to a man of the smallest culture, and *next,*—one in which he will be at the utmost disadvantage as regards the due discharge of his spiritual duties? If parents think twice now before they encourage a son's vocation to Holy Orders, will they ever think at all of exposing him to such a prospect as they will see before him under the altered state of things? As things now are there is at least respectability, and there is at least the certainty of a clergyman's being able to do some useful work for God and for his fellow-men. As the Archbishop would make things, there will be neither pay, position, nor peace. The average of the clerical character must sink. It is on the average, not on its few illustrious specimens, that the standing of any profession rests. And with the sinking of the average will come next the worthlessness and weakness of the institution. The Establishment will not be worth keeping up, and will fall before any, even the slightest blow.

We have purposely limited our remarks to the question of the Establishment, because *that* we presume is the point of view in which secular statesmen and peers of Parliament will look at it; and because we do not suppose that our own readers will require any remarks of ours upon the distinctively Church or spiritual aspect of the matter. We write thus, too, because unless he is much misrepresented, and indeed unless he much misrepresents himself, the Primate of All England is above all things zealous for the Establishment of which he is the most exalted member. He professes to act as he does in the interests of the Establishment, and we thoroughly believe in his personal sincerity. But we believe, also, that in the course upon which he has embarked, and into which he has persuaded his suffragans at least to seem to concur, he and they are but furnishing another illustration of our LORD's words as to what will happen to those who seek to save their lives. Seek to save the *Establishment* to the neglect of the *Church* and you will inevitably lose it. This is what the Archbishop is doing. *We* do not undervalue the uses of an Establishment. On the contrary, it is our fear that, though the Church of

CHRIST in England would survive the fall of the Establishment, yet that for a long time after we should have such a flood of irreligion as would appal the bravest. *We do not undervalue the Establishment.* But we value it in its place : as a means, not as an end. And we believe that the way to preserve the Establishment is to go straight on doing what is right, and not trimming our sails according to the popular clamour of mere Establishment-men. An Establishment policy will never save the Establishment. A Church policy assuredly will. Or if it should not, it will only be because the Establishment is no longer necessary to the Church. And it is because the course which the Archbishop is taking is so entirely an Establishment policy that we distrust it so utterly, even apart from the curious ingenuity of its blunderings. His Grace seeks to make things pleasant to " the nation," and selects as the parochial representatives of " the nation," not the majority of the Communicants of the Church, but "any three" residents to be those whom the parson must " satisfy." What a compliment to " the nation," if we could get into one assembly any number of these sets of three who are likely to come to the front in answer to this appeal, and set them forth as its representatives. Fancy, if the Bill were made a little more inclusive, and that " any three " were to be at liberty to complain of any inaccuracy in His Grace's way of performing Divine Service—say at the Consecration of a Bishop. Yet why not? Surely it is quite as important *to the Church* that an Archbishop should carefully obey her rules and rubrics on such an important occasion as that some obscure incumbent should observe the rubrics in his parish ministrations. But no. It is not *the Church* that His Grace is thinking of. It is the Establishment, and that particular section of "the nation" which cares the least possible about *the Church*. We grieve to have to write thus. But is it not simply—nay, conspicuously—true? And what is it all for? Why the whole number of cases in which any excess of ritual has taken place is absolutely unimportant, and, so far as any of them have been culpable, who can deny that they have been let alone, *in their inception*, by the Bishops themselves, who, *while things were beginning*, might have kept things straight by personal influence. It is all very well for the Bishop of Peterborough to make his jokes about Hophni and Phinehas—he forgets that he is invoking on himself the doom of Eli—but we had seen and known something of Diocesan administration long ere his Lordship quitted his non-parochial pulpits at the Octagon and at Quebec Chapel, and we do most positively assert that where the Bishop really oversees his Diocese, the *upgrowth* of any real *anomia* is not so easy. When the Bishop lets things alone—in plain words, if he gives random young men plenty of rope—there, no doubt, scandals may arise, and then, when they have grown up, they are difficult to uproot. But we object most strongly to ruining the Church of England just because of a few such cases which never ought to have existed. The very demand which the Archbishop makes is a confession that the office of the Bishop, his paternal and domestic supervision, was not exercised when it might have been.   It is our earnest hope, nay, it is our belief, that the present danger may be escaped. But it is a very painful thing for a loyal Churchman to feel that, but for our Official Chiefs having the opportunity of introducing a Bill into the House where there are no clergy to rise in reply, such a danger could not have been incurred.

C. W. REYNELL, PRINTER, LITTLE PULTENEY STREET, W.

www.ingramcontent.com/pod-product-compliance
Lightning Source LLC
Chambersburg PA
CBHW082059070426
42452CB00052B/2748